Egg-Laying Animals

Diana Noonan

Egg-Laying Animals

Text: Diana Noonan
Publishers: Tania Mazzeo and Eliza Webb
Series consultant: Amanda Sutera
  Hands on Heads Consulting
Editor: Sarah Layton
Project editor: Annabel Smith
Designer: Leigh Ashforth
Project designer: Danielle Maccarone
Diagram and map: Amanda Shufflebotham
Permissions researcher: Liz McShane
Production controller: Renee Tome

Acknowledgements
We would like to thank the following for permission to reproduce
copyright material:

Front cover: Alamy Stock Photo/InkaOne; pp. 1, 22: iStock.com/alexeys;
p. 4 (left): Shutterstock.com/Uwe Beckmann, (right): Alamy Stock Photo/
John Cancalosi; p. 5 (top left): iStock.com/Fgorgun, (top right): iStock.com/
Moonstone Images, (bottom left): Shutterstock.com/Worraket, (bottom
right): iStock.com/Jarrod Calati; pp. 6 (main), 23: iStock.com/
JohnCarnemolla; p. 6 (inset): iStock.com/Rejean Bedard; p. 7 (main):
Alamy Stock Photo/David Tipling Photo Library, (inset): Alamy Stock
Photo/Nature Picture Library; p. 8 (top middle), p. 24 (left): Alamy Stock
Photo/SBS Eclectic Images, (top right): Alamy Stock Photo/Dorling
Kindersley ltd, (bottom left, bottom middle), p. 24 (right): Alamy Stock
Photo/The Natural History Museum, (bottom right): iStock.com/
bigtunaonline; p. 9 (left): naturepl.com/Stefan Christmann, (right): Alamy
Stock Photo/Minden Pictures; p. 10 (top left): iStock.com/skynavin,
(top right): iStock.com/Luca Bertalli, (bottom left), back cover (top):
iStock.com/ShaneMyersPhoto, (bottom right): Shutterstock.com/
DSlight_photography; p. 11 (top): iStock.com/Placebo365, (bottom):
iStock.com/Dody Karyanto; p. 12 (main): Alamy Stock Photo/Ken Griffiths,
(inset): iStock.com/Casanowe; p. 13: Alamy Stock Photo/M. Timothy
O'Keefe; p. 14 (left), back cover (bottom right): Shutterstock.com/panpilai
paipa, (right): iStock.com/Nigel Marsh, (bottom): Alamy Stock Photo/
blickwinkel; p. 15 (top): naturepl.com/SCOTLAND: The Big Picture,
(bottom): Alamy Stock Photo/Martin Almqvist; p. 16 (left): iStock.com/
Mark Kostich, (right): Shutterstock.com/William Cushman, (bottom):
iStock.com/Clark Warren; p. 17 (top): Alamy Stock Photo/Anton Sorokin,
(bottom): iStock.com/Patrick Honan; p. 18 (left): Shutterstock.com/
Wirestock Creators, (right), back cover (bottom left): iStock.com/
ElementalImaging, (bottom): Alamy Stock Photo/BIOSPHOTO; p. 19 (top):
Shutterstock.com/sunipix55, (bottom): Nature In Stock/Bert Pijs;
p. 20 (main): Alamy Stock Photo/Dave Watts, (inset): Alamy Stock Photo/
imageBROKER.com GmbH & Co. KG.

Every effort has been made to trace and acknowledge copyright.
However, if any infringement has occurred, the publishers tender their
apologies and invite the copyright holders to contact them.

NovaStar

ISBN 978 0 17 033414 3

Cengage Learning Australia
Level 5, 80 Dorcas Street
Southbank VIC 3006 Australia
Phone: 1300 790 853
Email: aust.nelsonprimary@cengage.com

For learning solutions, visit **cengage.com.au**

Printed in China by 1010 Printing International Ltd
1 2 3 4 5 6 7 28 27 26 25 24

*Nelson acknowledges the Traditional Owners and Custodians
of the lands of all First Nations Peoples. We pay respect
to Elders past and present, and extend that respect to
all First Nations Peoples today.*

Contents

Which Animals Lay Eggs?

Some animals lay eggs. Their **young** grow inside the eggs. The outer layer of the eggs protects the young as they grow.

When the young are big enough to live on the outside, they hatch out of the eggs.

Many egg-laying animals build nests or choose safe **sites** for their eggs. Some egg-layers use their bodies to **incubate** their eggs.

Egg-laying animals include birds, reptiles, fish, **amphibians**, insects and **monotremes**.

budgerigar

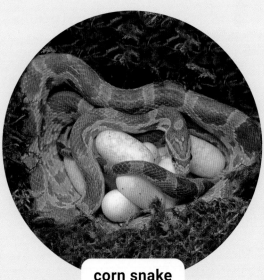

corn snake

Some egg-layers watch over their eggs and look after their young when they have hatched. But many leave their eggs after they have been laid.

clownfish

blue poison dart frog

banded peacock butterfly

short-beaked echidna

Birds

Birds are warm-blooded, egg-laying animals with feathers.

Birds that build nests use a variety of different materials, which help to keep their eggs warm. These include twigs, feathers, mud, wool, **moss** and even plastic!

This bird, a common loon, makes its nest from mud and grasses.

The willie wagtail uses spiderwebs to hold its nest together and make it warm.

Birds that don't build a nest choose a special nesting site where other animals can't see or reach their eggs.
It may be a rocky ledge, a branch, or a place in the grass or on the sand.

Some birds, such as the common murre (say: *mer*), nest on rocky ledges close to the sea. The murre's eggs are pointed at one end. This special shape helps stop the eggs rolling off the ledge.

A group of common murres nest on a rocky cliff.

A common murre pair get ready to incubate their egg.

Most birds lay a **clutch** of eggs in spring. Some birds lay more than one clutch of eggs each year.

Birds' eggs come in different shapes and sizes. The ostrich lays the largest egg in the world. Its eggs are around 15 centimetres long.

The smallest bird egg in the world is around 1 centimetre long (about the size of a jelly bean). It is laid by the bee hummingbird.

Different Shapes and Sizes of Bird Eggs

bee hummingbird egg
1.25 × 0.85 cm

common murre egg
8.2 × 5 cm

kiwi egg
12 × 8 cm

emperor penguin egg
12 × 8 cm

emu egg
13 × 9 cm

ostrich egg
15 × 12.5 cm

Most birds incubate their eggs by sitting on them. But some birds have unusual ways of incubating their eggs.

The female emperor penguin lays an egg, and then the male emperor penguin incubates it on top of his feet. He covers the egg with a warm, feathery layer of skin, called a "brood pouch".

A Sneaky Trick!

The shining cuckoo lays its eggs in other birds' nests to trick them into incubating the eggs for it.

A male emperor penguin incubates an egg.

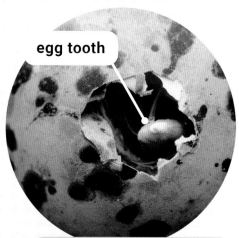

egg tooth

A chick uses its egg tooth to break out of its egg.

When a baby bird, or chick, is ready to hatch, it breaks open its shell with a small, hard piece of skin on its beak. This special "egg tooth" usually disappears as the chick grows.

Reptiles

Reptiles are cold-blooded animals. Their skin is covered in scales or horny plates. Common reptiles include snakes, lizards, turtles and crocodiles.

green tree python

chameleon

Hawaiian green sea turtle

saltwater crocodile

Most reptiles lay eggs, but some give birth to live young.

Some reptiles build a nest for their eggs, but most choose a special nesting site. Nesting sites include **hollows** in the sand, piles of leaves, and burrows.

Many reptiles guard their eggs once they have been laid. Some reptiles cover their eggs. The female saltwater crocodile covers her eggs with twigs, grass and mud.

A Chinese water dragon guards her eggs.

Saltwater crocodiles cover their eggs with nest materials like grasses to keep them safe and warm.

All reptiles lay their eggs on land, even those that spend most of their time living in water. They choose warm places because it helps the eggs to incubate.

Some pythons provide extra warmth for their eggs by shivering against them. When the python shivers, the eggs move a little, and this helps to warm them up.

A baby crocodile hatches from an egg.

The Australian diamond python curls around its eggs and shivers to warm them.

Most reptile eggs have a soft, **leathery** shell, but some have hard shells.

Lizards lay the smallest number of eggs in each clutch. Crocodiles and turtles lay the greatest number of eggs. Some turtles lay more than a hundred eggs in one clutch.

A Changing Climate

Sea turtles lay their eggs in the sand. If the sand is hotter than normal, the young will be female. As **climate change** heats Earth, there may be more female than male sea turtles.

Sea turtle babies break out of their eggs.

Fish

Fish are cold-blooded animals that live in the water.
Some fish give birth to live young, but most fish are egg-layers.

Some fish choose nesting sites such as empty shells,
the underside of rocks, and holes in muddy banks.

Male betta fish make a
bubble nest for their eggs.

The Port Jackson shark
lays a spiral–shaped egg.

A Sticky Nest

Some male fish
build nests. The male
stickleback builds a
nest from plants stuck
together with **fluid**
from his body.
Then, he dances to
attract a mate.

Fish can lay hundreds of eggs in one clutch. Some fish lay their eggs in nests, whereas others lay their eggs in **open water**.

Atlantic salmon eggs

The Atlantic salmon lives in the ocean. But it can swim a **route** of up to 2000 kilometres to lay its eggs in the same river where it hatched. Rivers are a more sheltered place for eggs than the ocean.

Atlantic salmon

An Atlantic Salmon Travel Route

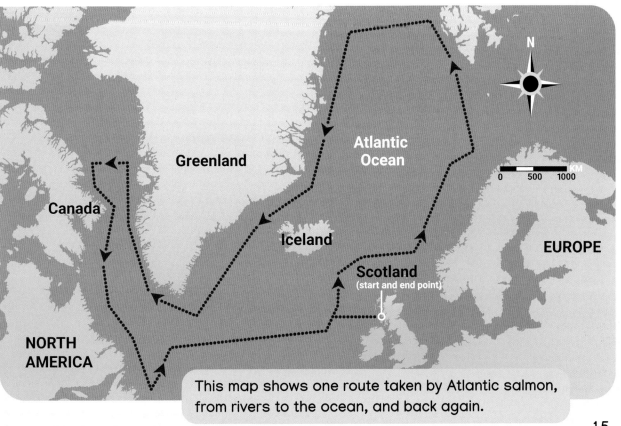

N

Greenland

Atlantic Ocean

KM
0   500   1000

Canada

Iceland

EUROPE

Scotland
(start and end point)

NORTH AMERICA

This map shows one route taken by Atlantic salmon, from rivers to the ocean, and back again.

Amphibians

Amphibians are cold-blooded, often smooth-skinned animals. Many of them are egg-layers. The most common amphibians are frogs. Axolotl are amphibians, too.

red-eyed tree frog

axolotl

Frog eggs have a slippery outer layer instead of a shell. The slippery layer helps to stop the eggs from drying out.

A clutch of frog eggs float in shallow water, which keeps them damp.

Frogs also keep their eggs damp by laying them in wet places, such as in or near water. Some lay their eggs under a leaf where the Sun cannot reach them.

The male glass frog guards the eggs until they hatch.

Waiting for Water

Frogs that live in the desert usually lay their eggs only after rain has fallen.

The desert tree frog can lay up to 300 eggs in one clutch after it has rained.

Insects

Insects are small, six-legged, winged animals. Some insects give birth to live young, but most are egg-layers.

carder bee

yellow jacket wasp

Some insects, such as bees, wasps and ants, build nests to hold their eggs. Others choose a site, such as the underside of a leaf or the inside of a stick.

Leaf-rolling insects, like the giraffe-necked weevil, roll up leaves and lay their eggs inside.

Insects usually lay their eggs close to food, so that the young can feed when they hatch. Some insects stick their eggs onto plants using a special "glue", which they make in their bodies.

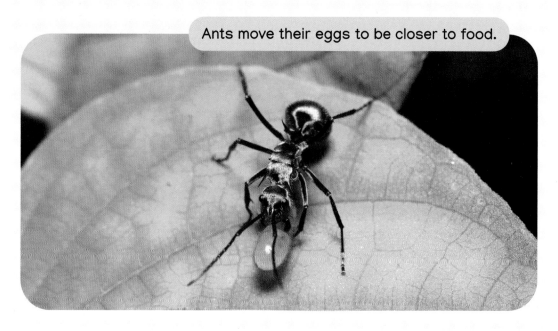

Ants move their eggs to be closer to food.

Safe and Sound

An earwig guards her eggs.

A female earwig guards her eggs and moves them if they're in danger. She licks her eggs to keep them clean and gathers them together if they scatter.

Monotremes

Monotremes are egg-laying **mammals** that produce leathery-shelled eggs. The only two monotremes are the echidna and the platypus.

A short–beaked echidna waddles across the ground.

The female platypus builds a nest of leaves and **grasses** in a burrow in the riverbank. She curls around her eggs to keep them warm.

A platypus comes out from its burrow in a riverbank.

The female echidna incubates one egg at a time in a pouch on her stomach. She makes milk in her body, which she feeds to her young.

How a Baby Echidna Hatches

Pouch House

Monotremes are the only egg-layers that make milk for their young, like mammals.

6

Living in the Burrow
The baby echidna lives with its mother until it is six months old.

5

Growing Spines
The baby's spines form after two months, and it leaves the pouch.

4

Growing Bigger
The baby echidna grows bigger in the pouch, but still has no spines.

3

Drinking Milk
The baby echidna drinks milk from the pouch hair.

2

Hatching the Egg
After incubating for 10 days in the pouch, the egg hatches.

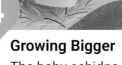

1

Laying an Egg
A female echidna lays an egg and puts it into her pouch.

Extraordinary Egg-Layers!

Egg-laying animals lay many different kinds of eggs. They lay them in the best place they can, and with the best shell or outer covering to keep them safe until the young are ready to hatch.

Egg-layers are among the most unusual and extraordinary animals in the world!

The blue robin lays bright–blue eggs.

An emu sits on a clutch of eggs.

Glossary

amphibians (*noun*)	animals that spend an equal amount of time on land and in water
clutch (*noun*)	a group of eggs laid at the same time
fluid (*noun*)	a liquid or flowing substance, like water
hollows (*noun*)	holes or empty spaces in the ground
incubate (*verb*)	to keep warm while something develops
leathery (*adjective*)	having a tough, hard surface
mammals (*noun*)	animals that give birth to live babies and feed them with milk
monotremes (*noun*)	animals that lay eggs and feed their babies milk
moss (*noun*)	a green plant that spreads over wet surfaces
open water (*noun*)	ocean or sea waters away from land
climate change (*noun*)	changes in weather patterns around the world
route (*noun*)	a way from one place to another
sites (*noun*)	places or locations
young (*noun*)	baby animals

Index